AND THE PRISONERS HEARD THEM

YOUR LIFE OF PRAISE CAN BRING FREEDOM TO OTHERS

By

SYLVIA M DALLAS

Text Copyright © 2014. Sylvia Dallas. All rights reserved

Photography by: Sylvia Dallas Photography

Book cover illustrated by: Carlene DeSilva

Published by: The Publisher's Notebook
email:PUBLISHER@thepublishersnotebook.com

International Standard Book Numbers:

- Ebook: 978-976-95691-2-6
- Hard Cover: 978-976-95691-0-2
- Paperback: 978-976-95691-1-9

All biblical references are from the King James Versions (KJV) unless otherwise indicated.

Quotations from The Passion Translation are indicated with the letters TPT

Quotations from New International Version are indicated with the letters NIV

DEDICATION

To the Holy Spirit for quickening me to write this book,

To my family, who gives me reason to praise God constantly

To Pastor Patrick Redwood – my spiritual mentor for many years especially for his gentle guidance.

And last but not least, to Michelle "Yapple Dapple" McKay, Vivienne Christie, Carol Henry and Pastor Courtney Morrison for encouragement

ENDORSEMENTS

This is true gold. Easy to read and yet so powerful. It is amazing what God can do through us. I feel built up, encouraged. Praise really does make it all better and God is truly awesome. All the mysteries of this world we cannot really understand, but the Word is truth and it's for each of us to discover it on our own. Thank you for sharing your work. The prayer at the end was everything.

Sandie Heron. (www.ourevidence.com)

*If there was ever an instructional literature on praise, **And The Prisoners Heard Them** should be considered as such, this book though small in stature, is very big on impact, the veracity of factual content fused with personal experiences put forth is unquestionably uplifting and nourishing for the spirit.*

Being the critic that I am, as I read through the chapters waiting to see where I would get bored and then discard the book, I somehow came to the realization that this might very well be the only book that I've started reading and finished it all in one go. Too often we are subjected to huge books from best -selling authors and the material is most often times gibberish and full of self praises and empty accolades, or at its best, repetition of existing material with no hint of freshness to captivate the mind.

And The Prisoners Heard Them is a timely reminder that one should always praise their way through the circumstances of life, quite frankly, you have no option but to reflect and analyze your daily walk with Christ and how often you give praise after perusing this work.

Sylvia has somehow managed to give us biblical factuality fused with her personal walk and the result of application of the word in thanks giving and praise even amidst the storms of life.

A must read for those of us who sometimes find it difficult to focus on God whilst going through turmoil.

Melvin Pennant (M.A.P)
Author: In My Time

PREFACE

I am always peacefully minding my own business when something happens.

So there I was peacefully minding my own business, listening to the sermon by Pastor Garth Rowe one Sunday evening, when I noticed something. He was giving a sermon on Praise unto Purpose and using the scripture reference Acts 16:25 and something jumped out at me – "and the prisoners heard them."

WOW! I had read this scripture many times, I have heard several sermons on this topic, I even recognized that when Paul and Silas prayed and praised, all the prisoners became free. I had only just recognized that the prisoners heard them. I remember texting my pastor and commenting that if the prisoners did not hear them, they would not have been freed also.

How does the manner in which I praise affect others? If I praise under my breath is it effective praise? What is my motive for praising God?

As I wrote this book, the Holy Spirit began to minister to me in a way I did not expect. At one point I had to pause and raise my hands in surrender and worship my Father. Tears streamed down my face in the open office, but I did not care. I thank Him for His ministry to me. I hope this book ministers to you also.

Sylvia Dallas

TABLE OF CONTENTS

<u>Prayer</u>

Father in Heaven, I pray that this book will be a blessing to those who read it. I pray that Your Holy Spirit will bring conviction to their spirit and that praises will emanate from them. I thank You for the spirit of obedience to write what you have put on my heart. May You be glorified by this work, in Jesus' precious name, Amen.

AND THE PRISONERS HEARD THEM

YOUR LIFE OF PRAISE CAN BRING FREEDOM TO OTHERS

SYLVIA M DALLAS

AND THE PRISONERS HEARD THEM

"And at midnight, Paul and Silas prayed and sang praises unto God: and the prisoners heard them" – Acts 16:25 KJV

Picture this. You are an unsaved person, and you keep hearing about this God that brings joy, peace and love. You have friends who say that they are Christians but you have yet to see any evidence of joy in their lives. All you can hear about is how difficult life is, they hardly ever smile and never have anything positive to say. Why on earth would you want to embrace the Christian life if this is the evidence of it?

As Christians we are supposed to be evangelizing, going out into the world and making disciples of all men according to the instructions we received in the Great Commission.[1] This means we are to preach the good news of the Gospel and drawing people to Christ. How can we achieve what is required of us if our spirits are downcast, if our countenance is low? Would you be attracted to the lifestyle of the person above? I think not!

Paul and Silas after being accused were locked in the deepest part of the dungeon and this was after they had just had "many stripes laid upon them " and

---

[1] Matthew 28: 19-20 KJV

"their feet fast in stocks"[2]. So beaten, placed in the inner part of the prison with their feet made immovable, they did the most unlikely thing...they began to pray and out of their prayers came praises which they sang unto God, doing the very thing for which they were jailed.

So you are in the dungeon, experiencing the similar conditions and a strange sound reaches your ears. "Who in their right mind could be singing in this place, at this time of the night?" "Are they aware that this is a prison?" "Isn't that sound coming from the innermost part of the prison where the worst punishment takes place?" Here you are in your most miserable of conditions and someone in a worst position is singing? At first, you would probably wonder if the conditions they are experiencing have gotten to their heads. As you listen, you realize this is not the crazy maniacal sound of someone slowly going off their rocker. This is pure unadulterated joy.

You cannot understand it, but as the sound penetrates your mind, it touches something deep inside of you and you listen. You want to catch the rhythm. Suddenly you find yourself swaying to the beat. You don't know the song but deep down something bubbles up inside of you. You feel as if there is a foaming fountain coming up from within your belly. As you continue to listen, a shout escapes you, you become somehow involved in what is happening and you feel tremors. Something earth shaking, soul shaking is

---

[2] Acts 16:22-24 KJV

taking place. You don't know what it is. You have never experienced anything like this before, but you definitely feel it and you know change is coming. Suddenly your chains are loosed, broken off of you, fallen to the ground.

Your praises to God are not just for you. Your praises need to be heard by others to bring deliverance to them. The praises to God from you cannot remain in your thoughts, they must come from the utterance of your lips to bring change to someone's life – not just yours. At the midnight of your life, beaten and chained to immovability, when you think that you are at rock bottom, you have no idea where the next meal is coming from, how you are going to make it the next day, facing life or death surgery, facing deathlike situations – trust God and praise Him.

Your praises can bring about the greatest move of evangelism in your life. Trials are always an opportunity to demonstrate God's power. When someone who is not saved sees you praising your way through your situations, sees you feeding yourself with the Word, sees the manifestation of God's peace in your life, they see you sleeping, unmoved by the storm and they wonder "how can I get some of that peace?" They move from "how can I" to "I want", and before you know it you are being asked "where do you go to church?"

Years ago, I went to visit a friend at her home. As the day passed and I was enjoying my time with her, there was a knock on the door. When she answered, there were about five policemen with a search warrant. I was told that I could not leave, nor was I allowed to make any calls. Well I just simply turned around, lay down on the carpet and went to sleep. This was not a restless, tossing and turning kind of sleep. This was deep comfortable, snoring kind of sleep. I woke up periodically and they were still there every time I woke up. The last time I woke up, one of the policemen asked me how come I am able to sleep. I told him that I was at peace because I know I was not involved in anything. He allowed me to leave.

When you praise, you are at rest. All the encumbrances become loosed from your life and the enemy can find nothing in you.

"And suddenly there was a great earthquake, so that the foundations of the prison were shaken; and immediately all the doors were opened, and everyone's bands were loosed." - Acts 16:26 KJV

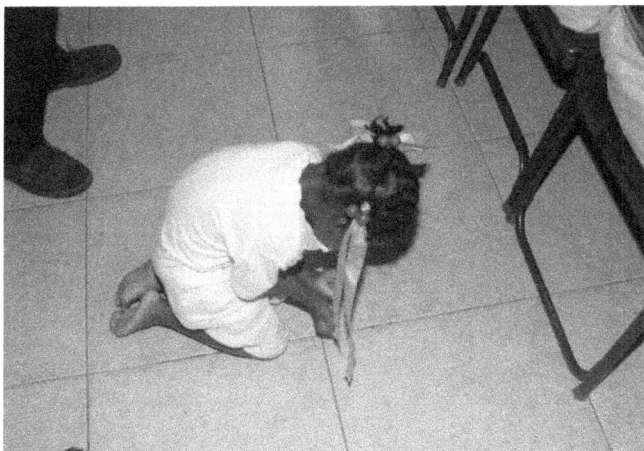

WHO ELSE SEES/HEARS YOUR PRAISE?

"Through the praise of children and infants, You have established a stronghold against Your enemies, to silence the foe and the avenger" Psalm 8:2 NIV

It is not only those who are distressed and in need of hope that sees your life of praise. Your enemies are thrown into confusion[3] when they realize that you are not fazed by what comes at you. You leave them wondering "why is this person so happy despite everything I am throwing at them?" You are not behaving according to what is expected of you. Instead of depression, there is joy. Instead of tears, there is laughter. Instead of complaining, there is a song on your lips.

---

[3] 2 Chronicles 20: 22 KJV

You are in a place where you cannot be touched.[4] The songwriter puts it this way:[5]

He will hide me, He will hide me,
Where no harm can e'er betide me;
He will hide me, safely hide me,
In the shadow of His hand.

Psalm 91 declares: "He that dwells in the secret place of the Most High, shall abide under the shadow of the Almighty." When you are in that secret place – nothing moves you. You are prepared to believe the promises of the Word of God no matter what you see happening around you. When His Word says "a thousand shall fall at thy side, and ten thousand on thy right hand; but it shall not come nigh thee"[6], you **ARE** believing that the God you serve is a God that cannot lie[7].

In 2 Chronicles 20 – King Jehoshaphat is faced with a dilemma. Three vast armies are coming against him. Is he fearful? Of course he is!! But does he allow fear to overcome him? No, instead he cries out to God for help. In the NIV version of the Bible it says in verse 3, "Alarmed, Jehoshaphat resolved to inquire of the Lord, and he proclaimed a fast for all Judah." *Alarmed* means he was experiencing a sudden fear, or distressing

---

[4] Psalm 91:1 KJV
[5] Words: Mary Servoss, 1878. Music: James McGranahan.
Title: He will hide me
[6] Psalm 91:6 KJV
[7] Numbers 23:19, Hebrews 6:18, Titus 1:2 KJV

suspense caused by an awareness of danger[8]. Despite feeling fearful, he decides to put the case for himself and the people of Judah before the heavenly court. "Are You not the God who is in heaven?" He declares his stand and the stand of the people, "If calamity comes upon us, whether the sword of judgment, or plague or famine, we will stand in Your Presence before this temple that bears Your Name, and will cry out to You in our distress, and You will hear us and save us".[9] The word *stand* in the Hebrew text was `amad (aw-mad')* which means to remain, to endure, to stop moving or doing, stand still, stand firm, maintain[10].

Here Jehoshaphat is declaring "no matter what the circumstance, no matter what happens, we are crying out to You, knowing that You hear us and depending on You to save us!" Can you come to that place? The place where you can say "though the seas roar and the earth moves[11], I am standing firm on this Rock and believing You for everything You say in Your Word?".

The rest of the story is history. The prophet declares to Jehoshaphat a word from God, "You will not have to fight this battle. Take up your positions; stand firm and see the deliverance the Lord will give you, Judah and Jerusalem. Do not be afraid; do not be discouraged. Go out to face them tomorrow, and the

---

[8] www.dictionary.com
[9] 2 Chronicles 20:6,9 NIV
[10] http://lexiconcordance.com/hebrew/5975.html
[11] Psalm 46:2 NIV

Lord will be with you.[12]" Upon receiving the Word, the king and the people of Judah and Jerusalem fell down and worshipped the Lord **IN A LOUD VOICE**. On the morning when they go to face the enemy, he appoints men to "sing to the Lord and to praise Him for the splendor of His Holiness."[13] Upon hearing the noise, the enemies are thrown into a state of confusion and kill each other.

God does not want us to hide from our enemies. He wants us to face them without fear, knowing that He is with us at all times. Indeed, if we live a life of praise we carry the Presence of God with us. So when we face our enemies in this confidence, they do not see us, they see Him.

"I will glory in the Lord at all times; His praise will always be on my lips. I will glory in the Lord, let the afflicted hear and rejoice. Glorify the Lord with me; let us exalt His name together" Psalm 34:1-3 NIV

---

[12] 2 Chronicles 20:17 NIV
[13] 2 Chronicles 20:21 NIV

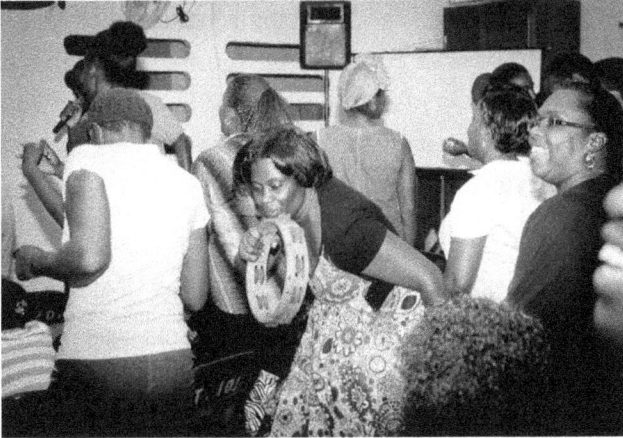

WHAT PRAISE DOES

"God's high and holy praises fill their mouths, for their shouted praises are their weapons of war!" Psalm 149:6 TPT

Our heartfelt praises to God brings down destruction upon the enemy. How many times have you felt depression lift from you as you lift your hands in surrender, focus on God and just praise Him? Have you not felt that sweet release that can come only from the deep recesses of your heart when you burst forth in song, shout a hallelujah, and just jump for joy because you trust God so much and believe on His word that His plans for you are to prosper you, to give you joy and hope for a future[14]? Therefore you understand what the Spirit of the Lord is telling you and anything else which contradicts that word must be a lie.

---

[14] Jeremiah 29:11 NIV

Your praises tell every spirit that is not of God –
"Look, I do not have time for you! You are subject to the
name of Jesus! At His name you must be subdued! You
must bow![15] For surely as I praise MY God, His glory will
come and you cannot abide here![16]"

Praise is our gateway to God.[17] For indeed as
we are saved from our enemies our deliverance
becomes a wall around us – a stronghold against the
enemy and our praise become our gates. *Violence will
disappear from your land; the desolation and
destruction of war will end". Salvation will surround you
like city walls, and praise will be on the lips of all who
enter there.*[18] Praise keeps the enemy OUTSIDE your
gates, so that when you see them forming their
weapons you can declare with all confidence "no
weapon formed against me shall prosper...for such is
my heritage"[19]

A wonderful result of praise, especially warfare
praise is the spoils thereof. In 2 Chronicles 20:25
something which is often overlooked happens. When
the people of Judah and Jerusalem went to where the
enemies were camped and saw that they were all dead,
they began to haul away the spoils or the treasures of
the enemy. It took them three days to "carry off their
plunder"[20]. On the fourth day, they assembled in the

---

[15] Philippians 2:10-11 NIV
[16] Psalm 24: 7-9
[17] Isaiah 60:18
[18] Isaiah 60:18 NLT
[19] Isaiah 54:17
[20] 2 Chronicles 20:25 NIV

Valley of Berakah and guess what they did!!! If you said praise the Lord, you would be absolutely correct. The scripture says that it is called the Valley of Berakah to this day.

So clap your hands! As you clap your hands[21], you strike[22] the enemy and blast them out of your way. Shout! Split the ears of the enemy! Let God arise with your shout![23] Tear down the stronghold that the enemy has built around with your shout!![24] When you dance you are trampling the enemy. You are declaring that the enemy is under your feet. You are affirming that the spirit of boldness is upon you and there is no fear. You were promised that you would be able to tread upon scorpions and snakes and nothing can in any way harm you[25].

Do you want your enemies to tremble? Do you want the mountains in your life to be moved? He has promised that He will shake heaven and earth for you.[26] Invite the Presence of God to be with you by living a life of praise. He inhabits the praises of His people.[27] When your enemies see that God will fight on your behalf,

---

[21] TERUW`AH (ter-oo-ah) alarm, signal, sound of tempest, shout, shout or blast of war or alarm or joy . Language: Hebrew; Source: Strong's 8643
[22] TAQA (taw-kah`) to blow, clap, strike, sound, thrust, give a blow, blast. Language: Hebrew; Source: Strong's 8528
[23] "God arises with the ear-splitting shout of His people!....." Psalm 47:5 TPT
[24] Joshua 6:16-20
[25] Luke 10:19
[26] Haggai 2:5-6 NIV
[27] Psalm 22:3 NLT

wisdom will come upon them, because of the fear of God.[28]

"O that You would rend the heavens and come down, that the mountains would tremble before You! As when fire sets twigs ablaze and causes water to boil, come down to make Your name known to Your enemies and cause nations to quake before you" – Isaiah 64: 1-2 NIV

---

[28] Proverbs 9:10

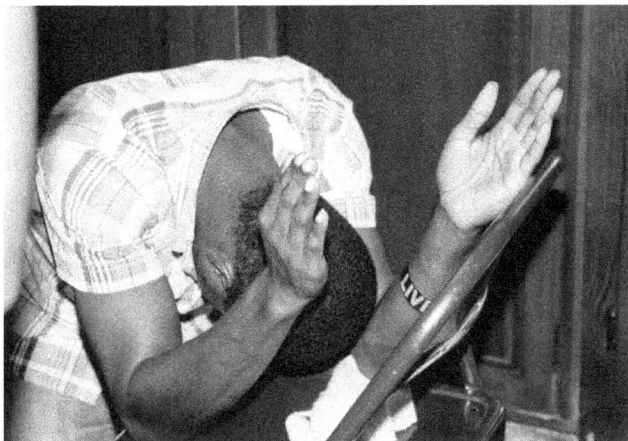

PRAISING THROUGH THE REFINING PROCESS

But who may abide the day of his coming? and who shall stand when he appeareth? for he is like a refiner's fire, and like fullers' soap: - Malachi 3:2 KJV

Now it is quite easy to praise God when things are good. Will you be like the Israelites in the wilderness? As soon as they faced a little difficulty, they started to murmur, they started to wish for the goodies they enjoyed without cost in Egypt,[29] they started to accuse God of taking them out into the desert to kill them.[30]

---

[29] Numbers 11:6
[30] Numbers 16:13

Somehow when we accept Jesus as our Lord and Saviour, we expect that things will get better overnight. We expect to be on easy street, sailing smoothly along without a care in the world. Wrong!! Do you think the enemy is going to let you go so easily? When you become saved, you have been pulled out of the darkness and into His marvelous light. The devil had no problem with you being in the darkness!!! He is going to put every stumbling block in your way. He is going to remind you of past sins, he is going to try to cause you to take offense to every little thing. In other words, he is going to pull out his bag of tricks and go at you like never before.

You might be tempted like the Israelites to say "before I got saved I never used to feel unhappy, I could enjoy myself anytime, I never had it so hard, life was easier." Was it? Did the Israelites really eat all they could for free? What about their life of slavery? How easy it becomes to forget that "little" detail. Were they crying out to God for deliverance because life was so easy[31]? I think not!!

I remember a dream I had once in which the devil himself came up to me with a scroll trailing behind him. Do you remember your cartoon days when the messenger comes before the king with a scroll and it trailed behind him for miles? Such was the scroll he carried. I listened politely while he read off the scroll of my past deeds. I was not rude as I had remembered the

---

[31] Exodus 3:7

scripture about Michael not daring to accuse him.[32] I simply waited until he was finished (I did not want him to have to come back with anything that was not covered on the list, because I had cut him off in mid-stream) and said "Behold! Old things are passed away, all things become new in Christ Jesus[33]." I reminded him that what he had in his hand was not the end of **my** book and that I knew the end of **his** book.

I could only have done this because I had the Word hidden in my heart and believed in it. Failing that I would have taken on a spirit of condemnation, and its accompanying friends. How do we benefit from trials? A seedling just out of the nursery cannot withstand constant watering. It needs to be buffeted by the wind, warmed by the sun and watered. Without the first two, the roots rot and the plant eventually dies. In the same way, if we were to get everything easily without going through out trials, we would begin to take those things for granted. If you can only praise God during the good times then you are only interested in the things that God can give you and not building a relationship with Him.

Imagine that you have someone that calls you friend, but the only time you see them is when they want something from you. Would that feel good? But if that person is your friend, they have a relationship with you, they seek your company all the time, and they plan things with you in mind.

---

[32] Jude 1:9
[33] 2 Corinthians 5:17

God is a gracious God. He will not refuse you the desires of your heart for He promised "Ask and it shall be given...[34]" There is so much more to God than using Him as a counter to go up to and say "gimme, gimme". When we seek the presence of God, when we seek a relationship with Him, when we come into the knowledge of who we are in Him, when we recognize that because of our inheritance as a **child** of God, we know we can interrupt the meeting with kings at any time. We can knock on the door of the conference room, put our head around the door and say "Abba my heart hurts, may I sit on your lap for a while?" We know without a doubt that He will say "come in my daughter/son, let me hold you for a while, let me heal the pain away." When we know THAT, we are in His Presence. Hallelujah!!!

In the secret place of His Presence, we see the storms around us and we can sleep. The earth is shaking, the waves ride high, but we are not moved. We have the confidence that our Father has our backs!! In His Presence there is joy and many pleasures at His right hand.[35]

The scripture in the epistle of James says "count it all joy when you experience diverse trials[36]" because it brings out the best in us. Sometimes the difficulties

---

[34] Matthew 7:7

[35] "For you bring me a continual revelation of overflowing life, The path that brings me to the overflowing joys; Of the exquisite and eternal pleasures of gazing upon Your face." Psalm 16:11 TPT

[36] James 1:2

we face are because of our own disobedience. Sometimes we have to face correction from God, but that does not mean He loves us less. The Lord disciplines those that He loves.[37] You might say, why would I have to be disciplined, love is not like that. Wrong!! God does not play favorites.[38] Nor does He go back on His Word. However, if we truly repent, He forgives.

For us to grow, we must face the difficulties of life. Is it not satisfying to know that you can obtain wisdom on how to deal with these situations by being close to the Father? The Passion Translation (TPT) of Psalm 16:6-9 puts it like this:

Your pleasant path leads me to pleasant places. I'm overwhelmed by the privileges that come from following You, for You have given me the best! The way You counsel and correct me makes me praise You more; For Your whispers in the night give me wisdom, showing me what to do next. Because You are close to me and always available, My confidence will never be shaken, For I experience Your wrap-around Presence every moment. My heart and soul explode with joy – full of glory! Even my body will rest confident and secure.

---

[37] Hebrews 12:6 NIV
[38] Acts 34:10

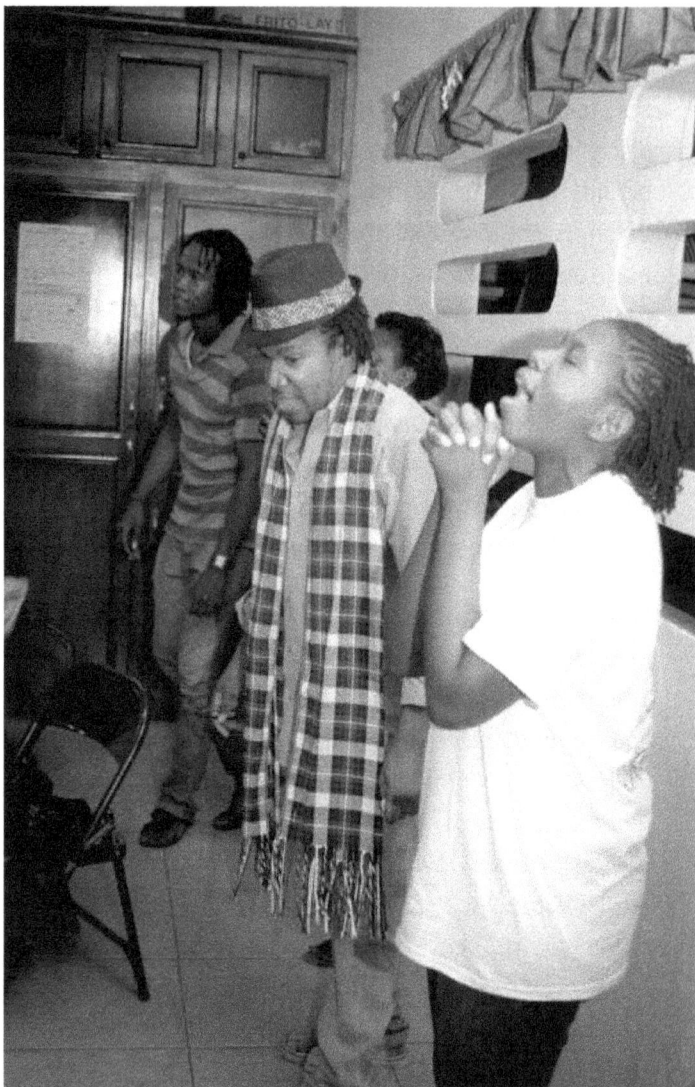

THE DYNAMIC DUO – PRAISE AND PRAYER

Then He spoke a parable to them, that men always ought to pray and not lose heart. - Luke 18:1 KJV

If we look again at Paul and Silas in their situation, we will notice that they did not grumble about their difficulty. They endured their beating, endured being placed in the stocks and I would imagine they might have passed out from the pain and suffering. It is a physically natural thing to happen. However, the pain had dulled a bit and they are now awake, night has come. If you can picture the stench, the dampness, the rats, the infestation, the cold – it is enough to make anyone lose heart and become discouraged. I can just imagine the conversation:

Paul: Silas how are you feeling?

Silas: I don't know which part of me does not hurt. What about you?

Paul: The same.

Silas: I think I just felt a kitten brush my leg

Paul: It was not a kitten. A kitten would run from that. I don't think you should focus on what's around you too much

Silas: Any ideas?

Paul: Let's practice what we preach, let's pray

How many times have you focused on your circumstances instead of praying[39]? When you pray, remind the Lord of His promises. The prophet Isaiah[40] says we should "take no rest" and give Him no rest until he establishes and makes Jerusalem a praise in the earth. The word Jerusalem means vision of peace.[41] In Isaiah also we are encouraged to remind God of His promises, to "state your case that you may be proved right"[42]

God is perfection itself. He does not forget His promises. Who benefits when we remind God of His promises? Of course it is us who benefit! As we pray and remember the goodness of God, His perfection, His purity, His constant Presence in our lives, His gentleness, His desire for a relationship with us, a fire is stoked in us. We feel a gladness come upon us. Suddenly circumstances no longer matter. We are caught up in His Presence, basking in His glory. Suddenly we are not paying attention to negative words, we are not believing the lies of the enemy. We are facing truth. We become sanctified by His truth because His word is truth.[43] In seeing the truth of our situation, we can overcome the facts. Yes it is a fact that you have a pain, but truth says that by His stripes you are healed[44]. So you do not see your healing yet,

---

[39] Psalm 62:1-2
[40] Isaiah 62:7 NIV
[41] Combined Bible Dictionary; Ref: Hitchcock's Bible Names Dictionary
[42] Isaiah 43.26 KJV
[43] John 17:17
[44] Isaiah 53:5, I Peter 2:24

but you believe the promises of your Father. Then fix your eyes on what you have not yet seen.[45] Now when you believe that what is not yet seen is more real than what is around you, what else can come out of your mouth but praise? There are more than enough people in the scriptures that demonstrate praising God in advance of seeing a victory. They believed God for the victory and that was enough reason to praise Him.

Jehoshaphat appointed Levites to sing unto the Lord in the beauty of His holiness based on a promise, but without seeing the victory first.

David continually praised God throughout his circumstances no matter what they were. He usually started out in prayer and ended up in praise.

Too often we are near sighted, seeing only the circumstances that are near. When we see the circumstances only they tend to become exaggerated. We start thinking about the "what-if's". Let's revisit the scene in the prison with Paul and Silas (remember this is conjecture). So Silas feels something brush against his foot. When Paul says "that's not a kitten", Silas remembers that he is afraid of rats. He starts to panic, (remember he cannot move), he breaks out in a sweat, he starts to think about the rat biting him and the possibility of him getting some disease. He starts to worry that he is going to die in this place. He starts to complain, "you know Paul if it was not for you bothering that girl with the divination spirit, we would not be in

---

[45] 2 Corinthians 4:18

this pickle. Couldn't you keep your temper in check? I would not have handled it that way … and now because of you we are in this hole." You see how the problem becomes magnified.

Now picture you being a prisoner and hearing that. Would that encourage you? I don't think so!!. Thank God that is not what happened or we would not have this great testimony right now! So let your praises of God be continually on your lips. When your circumstances threaten to overcome you like a flood remember that the Lord will raise up a standard against them.[46] Be like David, no matter what the circumstance say:

"Lord! I am bursting with joy over what you have done for me! My lips are full of perpetual praise. I am boasting of You and all Your works, so let all who are discouraged take heart" – Psalm 34:1-2 TPT

---

[46] Isaiah 59:19 KJV

T HE THREEFOLD CORD – PRAYER, PRAISE AND FASTING
"…..a threefold cord is not easily broken" Eccl. 4:12

We have talked about prayer, praise and the effects of combining them. Have you ever thought about the triple combo? "What's the triple combo?" you might ask. You have been introduced to the dynamic duo in the previous chapter. It's time to meet the last member of the super team.

"As they ministered to the Lord, and fasted, the Holy Ghost said, Separate me Barnabas and Saul for the work whereunto I have called them.[47]" Imagine that! Out of praise, prayer and fasting, the Holy Spirit comes and directs your path. Awesome!!!

---

[47] Acts 13:2 KJV

What is fasting? Is it just starving yourself for a period of time? Is it something that must be endured? Is it to show others, "look at me, see how I am suffering for the Lord?" In this scripture "as they ministered to the Lord" means as they worshipped and prayed to the Lord. The Greek for the word ministering in this scripture is *leitourgounton* (nope, I cannot pronounce it), which means officiating.[48] This means that they were performing the duty of priests which was to minister to God through prayer and worship. In addition to ministering before the Lord, they fasted.

Fasting is the discipline of humbling ourselves before God. Before every major event that occurs in the Bible there is a period of separation unto God, a period of fasting. It is a time in which God was actively sought for direction and purpose. A time of humbling, recognizing that to win this battle, overcome this difficulty, climb this hurdle – it is not the strength of man that will prevail but the will and purpose of God[49]. *Then I proclaimed a fast there, at the river of Ahava, that we might afflict ourselves before our God, to seek of him a right way for us, and for our little ones, and for all our substance. – Ezra 8:21-23.* Here Ezra clearly states what the purpose of his fast was. Not just seeking guidance for the adults, but for the children and all that they possessed.

48

http://www.scripture4all.org/OnlineInterlinear/NTpdf/act13.pdf
[49] Zechariah 4:6

An often quoted scripture with regards to fasting is Isaiah 58: 1-14. In this scripture, the Lord speaks about how fasting should be. In our fasting we should not seek justice while we dispense injustice, praying for the repentance of others while we coddle the hidden sins within us. If our voices are to be heard on high, we have to come clean before God. We cannot be looking to take the mote of someone's eye while we have a beam in ours[50].

The purpose of your fast must be to:
- Free the imprisoned
- Feed the hungry
- Clothe the naked
- Embrace your own flesh and blood

You can ask the Lord to free you from the bars that imprison you, feed your hungry soul with His word, clothe your nakedness in His righteousness, and cleanse you from all unrighteousness. In this time of humbling yourself, feel free to place everything that is not of Him upon the altar for His consuming fire. The Lord will honor your sacrifice and your willingness to humble yourself before Him.

He promises in this same word that:
- Your healing will come
- You will be glowing with health and vitality
- Your righteousness will go before you (God is your righteousness)[51]

---

[50] Matthew 7:3
[51] Jeremiah 23:6

- The glory of the Lord will be your rear guard
- You will call and He will answer
- You will cry for help and He will say "here am I"
- If you do away with the wickedness of your heart and deeds;
  - the gossiping,
  - the malicious behavior,
  - oppressing others

If you work on behalf of the hungry and satisfy the needs of the oppressed:

- He will guide you always
- Satisfy your needs even during the harsh times
- Strengthen you
- You will be like a well-watered garden, like a spring that never dries
- You can rebuild that which was demolished
- You can repair the broken walls (your salvation)
- You can close the breaches (any gateway where the enemy gained a foothold)

Fasting with prayer and praise must bring deliverance. Fasting causes the fire of God to fall in your life and in your church. Throughout the bible it was seen that fasting was the primary means of humbling ourselves before God. Fasting – denying our flesh declares:

- I am not living by bread alone, but by every Word that proceeds out of the mouth of God[52]
- I want to hear clearly from God[53]. The angel told Daniel that from the **first day** he decided to humble himself and pray, that the Lord heard him and sent an answer.
- I have a very real need to be guided by the Holy Spirit and will depend only on God.

When you press in to seeking the things of God through prayer and fasting, you must hear from God and praise must come as a result. When you cry out to Him through prayer and fasting, He will say "here am I". What a promise!!!

Humbling ourselves before God can only bring about humility of spirit. It brings about brokenness, contriteness and repentance. God will not despise a contrite heart[54]. In our brokenness, when we confess our sins and repent of them, the Lord will deliver us with His great right arm. When we fast we receive cleansing from our sins by effective repentance[55], a renewal of our spirit and help in any situation that we might face. Our fasting is a way of waiting on the Lord. He has promised that when we wait on Him, he will

---

[52] Deuteronomy 8:3
[53] Daniel 10:12
[54] Ps 51:17
[55] II Chronicles 7:14

renew our strength, we shall soar like eagles, we shall run and not get tired, we shall walk and not faint[56].

God wants us to return to Him in fasting and prayer. He is not asking for an open display (for man to see) of us rending our garments, but our hearts[57]. Once we are free of the encumbrances of our soul, we cannot help but worship Him in Spirit and in Truth.[58]

"The LORD is near to all who call on him, to all who call on him in truth" – Psalm 148:18

---

[56] Isaiah 40:31
[57] Joel 2:12-13
[58] John 4:24

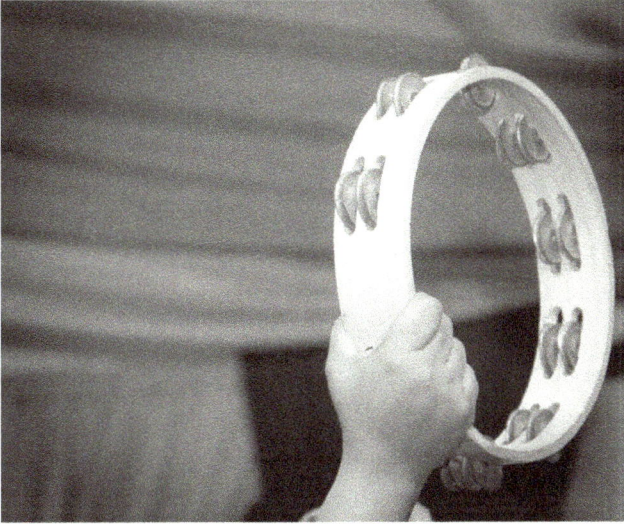

GLORIFYING GOD THROUGH A LIFE OF PRAISE

May my lips overflow with praise, for you teach me your decrees. Psalm 119:171

We have seen the importance of prayer, praise and fasting in the preceding chapters. How can we apply this to our lives? In the epic battles of the Bible, when the Israelites moved under the direction of God, it was always the Levites (the high priests) who led the way or the Lord would say "Send Judah first[59]." The name Judah means "praise Yahweh" or "may God be praised". Do you remember Leah in the book of Genesis? Even though she got married to Jacob first, she was not secure in his love. In fact, she was painfully aware of the fact that her father tricked Jacob in to

---

[59] Judges 1:1-2; 20:18

marrying her. Upon realizing that she could not secure his love even though she bore him three sons, she finally stopped striving for his favor. When she bore Judah she said "this time I will praise the Lord"[60].

In the Gospel according to John, we see where Mary Magdalene sacrificed the most valuable thing she had, and anointed Jesus' feet. We are told that the room was filled with the fragrance of her offering.[61] In the song "Alabaster Box" by CeCe Winans, she declares the perfume in the box to be her praise. Does the perfume of your praise fill the room, fill the atmosphere, fill the heavenlies, no matter what you are going through? In every battle we face, our praises must come up to God as a sweet smelling savor. We are able to praise Him even in the difficult circumstances because we know who He is and who we are to Him.

The word praise in any language speaks of high esteem and value. The Old French word *preisier* means to value, the Late Latin *pretiare* – which means to esteem highly, or the Latin Word *pretium* which means prize or precious. In good old English it means to "express commendation, admiration" or to proclaim or describe the glorious attributes of (a deity) with homage and thanksgiving".[62]

Think about this. Angels see the glory of God, they are in His Presence constantly, they cannot help but worship Him. When we worship in the midst of our

---

[60] Genesis 29:35
[61] John 12:3
[62] http://dictionary.reference.com/browse/praise?s=t

trials, without seeing His glory, without seeing the expected end yet, at the beginning of the battle even when we do not know what the outcome will be, this is worship in spirit and in truth[63]. How can we help but touch the Father's heart when we give our all and worship in this way?

Everything about our lives must be pleasing to our Father. When our lives are seen to be victorious, we help the other prisoners who are listening to what we say.

Praise must be expressed. There is no such thing as being dignified about our praise. The word itself suggests exuberance, excitement, pleasure. God is not saying that we must not face the fact of what is happening to us, but truth (which is Jesus Christ Himself[64]) trumps fact any day. Truth is an overcomer of every kind of evil. This truth should make us jump for joy, shout with happiness and laugh with exuberance. This truth is our strong tower, our defense, our cleft in the Rock, our fortress, our security. Our trials should make us cling to this truth even more. If we know the promises of our Father and believe them, how can we not have a joyous life?

I remember a time when I was going through what I call a "no money trial". I clung tenaciously to Isaiah 3:10. I said "Lord, Your word says, no bread, no water, trials etc, but Isaiah 3:10 says tell the righteous it

---

[63] Adapted from: The Call (The Final Quest Series) by Rick Joyner
[64] John 14:6

31

will be well with them... and since I know that my righteousness is like filthy rags and I am seeking constantly after Your righteousness... I know without a doubt, You won't leave me hungry. So I thank You for even this trial, for I know you are going to work this situation for my good." Every morning that I woke up, I just praised Him. If the situation got to be more than I could bear and I could not sing, I would put on worship music so that I would maintain an atmosphere of praise until I could start singing.

Now I am sure that some of my neighbors must think I am mad. Even during my very sick days, I still managed to squeak out a hallelujah. The prophetic singers of Korah's clan had the perfect remedy "Why are you in despair, O my soul? And why have you become disturbed within me? Hope in God, for I shall again praise Him for the help of His presence...[65]" To them, the Presence of God was enough, was help. Why be downcast indeed? If the enemy comes at you like a flood, surely you already know that the Lord will raise a standard against him?

Feeling worthless? Remind yourself that you are God's masterpiece[66], that He knows every hair on your head[67], that you are fearfully and wonderfully made[68], you are the apple of His eye[69]. Think back to the times that He has brought you through. Eagerly

---

[65] Psalm 42:5-6
[66] Ephesians 2:10
[67] Luke 12:17, Matthew 10:30
[68] Psalm 139:14
[69] Psalm 17:8

shout out what you remember of His abundant goodness and speak joyfully of His righteousness[70]!

Feeling fearful? Because you are the apple of His eye, He will take it personally when anyone touches you and cause even those less than your enemies to destroy them.[71] Take courage, you were not given a spirit of fear but of love, power and a sound mind.[72] You are His battle-axe, His weapon of war[73]. In Him you can run through troops and leap over walls[74], you can tear up the gates of your bondage from its foundation[75]. You are mighty through Christ!!

So shout, laugh, clap, sing, dance. Do not concern yourself with whether or not people are going to look at you strangely. You are doing this to glorify God. He is the only audience you should be focused on. But when others who are feeling imprisoned by despondency, anger, fleshly desires, who lack joy, hope and love, see you praising your way through your adversities, do not be surprised if you hear the question, "What church do you go to?"

---

[70] Psalm 147:7
[71] Zechariah 2:8
[72] II Timothy 1:7
[73] Jeremiah 51:20
[74] II Samuel 22:30
[75] Judges 16:1-3

PROLOGUE

Behold, what manner of love the Father hath bestowed upon us, that we should be called the sons of God; therefore the world knoweth us not, because it knew Him not. 1 John 3:1 KJV

All of what I wrote previously will not mean a hill of beans to you if you do not know Christ. As the scripture above indicates, if you are of the world, you know Him not.

I got saved when I was ten years old. I heard a preaching on the bus and asked Jesus to come into my heart and be Lord and Saviour. I had no access to teaching, so I "winged" it as best I could. I was always in a battle with my spirit – for indeed the things of the flesh does war with the things of the spirit[76]. Being sexually abused from a young age, I battled with the issue of lust for most of my life. I straddled the divide of spirit and flesh for 36 years of my life. It was a roller coaster ride of triumph and defeat, which I truly could have done without. In reality I had no excuse, I could have sought knowledge, I was rebellious, I rationalized all the wrong things I did, yet I had no peace. In 2011, I recommitted myself to God, giving myself wholeheartedly to Him and making a decision to be obedient to His word and the promptings of His Holy Spirit. I have never regretted it and I now truly understand the term "the peace that passeth all understanding".

---

[76] Galations 5:17

Do you feel a yearning for something deeper? Do you want to live this life of praise? Are you saying to yourself even as you go to the night club for the umpteenth time on a Friday or Saturday night, and come home feeling empty, "there must be more?" I am not promising you an easy life. I am promising a life of adventure with God. I am promising that if you allow Him to lead you, you will never be bored. I am promising that as you face trials with the certainty of the promises of God to stand on, that He will never disappoint you. Are you ready? What is stopping you at this moment? Are you feeling that you need to clean up your life first? What if I told you that you will never be able to clean up your life without the help of the Holy Spirit? The Lord is inviting you – "come as you are". In Isaiah 1:18 – He says, "come let us reason together, for though your sins be as scarlet, they will be as white as snow….."

If you feel this yearning, this tugging on your heart to know Christ, now is your time for salvation. He can give you the peace you seek, heal your wounds, help you to forgive, love you unconditionally. Are you ready? You cannot come to God unless you come through Jesus Christ.[77] Let's pray:

Father in Heaven, I come before You confessing my sins, agreeing with You that I am a sinner. I believe that Your son Jesus died for those sins. I believe that His blood cleanses me of all unrighteousness. I confess and accept Jesus as my Lord and Saviour right now. I repent

---

[77] John 4:16

of every sin against You and believe that all my sins are now forgiven. I believe that I am a new creation in Jesus. I now receive His healing in my life for all my pains and sorrows by faith and believe that all those burdens have been lifted from me. I thank You and entrust the full control of my life to You from now on. In Jesus' name – Amen.

Yes, it is that easy. God did the hard part through Jesus Christ for us already. Would you have had the willingness to sacrifice your only son as payment for all the sin of mankind? No matter what you may have purposed in your heart to make this sacrifice, I guarantee, you would not have followed through. But Jesus in the Garden of Gethsemane, even though He knew what was coming, knew the suffering He would go through, knew that His beloved Father would not be able to look at Him because He would become sin said, "....yet not My will but Yours.[78]"

You have confessed with your mouth the Lord Jesus, and believe that God raised Him from the dead, therefore you are saved.[79]

Your next step is to find a full gospel church in your area and attend bible study classes as well as services. Do not think it is okay to just stay home and tune in to a radio or television program. The Word of

---

[78] Luke 22:42
[79] Romans 10:9

God says that we should not forsake the fellowship.[80] Welcome to the victorious life!!

".....there is rejoicing in the presence of the angels of God over one sinner who repents." – Luke 15:10 NIV

Declaration of Praise

My Father in heaven, I thank You for all that You are in my life. I thank You that You love me so much that You are concerned about every detail of my life. Help me to live a life that is pleasing to you and teach me Your ways, so that I may know You and continue to find favor with You.

I acknowledge that You are the source of my happiness, my finances, my everything. In You I live, in You I breathe, in You I have my being. I thank You for creating me as the pinnacle of Your creation, in Your image and likeness to have dominion and stewardship over all that You have created.

I acknowledge that You are the God of wonders, of majesty, of dominion and power. I know that Your hand is not too short to accomplish anything that may seem impossible to me. As a result, I know without a doubt that You cover me under Your wings because I have found the peace of Your secret place.

I acknowledge You as my Banner, my Shepherd, the Mighty Warrior who fights on my behalf. Who dares to stand against me when You stand before me? I declare

---

[80] Hebrews 10:23-25

that though circumstance may raise its ugly head to try to defeat me, I know who my Redeemer is.

I lay myself bare before You O God, because You are He who searches the mind and heart. You are my Ever Present Help in time of trouble, my Wisdom in any situation. You are my Bastion of help, my Refuge, my Strong Tower. You are my Healer, my Anointing Oil, my Deliverer. Your Word is meat to my bones. Your Spirit is water to my thirsty soul. You are the Oasis in the wilderness. You are the Light which illuminates the dark places in my life. You are the Prince of Peace.

You are merciful and longsuffering, loving, forgiving and holy. My desire is to be a true reflection of You. You are the still gentle voice that guides me, the thunder that makes my enemies quake. You are my Rock, my firm foundation.

You are my Righteousness, my Sanctification, my Salvation. You are my Way, my Truth and my Life. You are my Judge, my Friend, closer than a brother.

My lips will not cease to praise Your Holy name. I will declare Your majesty and Your glory always.

Selah.

Love Encounter

My heart quickens
It feels as if it would burst
So overcome with passion
Wrought from an encounter with You

I lean into your embrace
As I rest my head
Upon Your bosom
The sound of Your heartbeats
Echoes
Reverberates
Like thunder

I feel
Vibrations
Pulsing
Throughout my body
And even into my spirit
As our heartbeats
Find a unified rhythm

Coming into agreement
Of a great union with You
My soul knows very well
It's real

It's trustworthy
This outpouring of love
From Your heart to mine

My spirit has caught on
To a divine rhythm
I am ruined for any other sound
Any other beat
I can never be the same again.

Come & See

I heard Him speak
And followed Him
And when He asked me
What was it that I sought
I said "Lord, show me where You live "
He said
"Come and see "

And I obeyed.

My joy in His presence
Could not be contained
I went seeking a friend
With whom to share
When I saw him I said
"I have found the Christ
Come and see "

I saw another friend
Who told me about Him
He said his heart listened
When Jesus said "Follow me "
And together we went
And told other friends
"We have found a
Good thing out of Nazareth

Come and see "
They who went to see Him

Realized that He already knew them
And each went to a friend
And proclaimed
"We have found Him
Who knew us
Him who redeemed us
Him who promised us
Open heavens because we believed

We found Him
Who stormed the gates of hell
And took back the keys!
Who heals the sick
Him who frees the oppressed
We have found Him
Who stills the storm
Walks on water
We have found Him!
We have found Him!
Come and see!"

About the Author

Sylvia M Dallas, born June 9, 1965 accepted Jesus Christ as her Lord and Saviour at the age of 10 years. It was at that time that she discovered her gift for writing. In 2000 she published her first book under the pseudonym Gina Rey Forest and several books later on. In 2007 she declared unto God, "I will not perform on stage again, or write another poem unless it glorifies You". She was immediately tested. She received several offers to perform her previous style of sensuous poetry with pay. She turned them all down. In 2011, she recommitted her life to God, promising to be obedient to His word and the promptings of His Holy Spirit. On January 1, 2014 she completed the manuscript of her first book of poetry since that commitment called The Right Kind of Intimacy. In March, as she was preparing to publish, and during a time of prayer, she was asked by the Lord if she would hold off publishing that book and instead publish another book that He would place on her heart to write. She agreed.

For feedback on this book you may contact her at: sylvia@sylviadallas.com. Twitter: @syldallas Facebook: www.facebook.com/sylviamdallas or visit her blog THE BETTER DIRECTION at http://sylviadallas.com
Telephone: (876) 833-6722